Leading by Listening

How to Deepen Connection
with Open Questions

JOHN ARNDT

©2025 Flourish Direction LLC

No part of this book may be reproduced in any form or by any electronic or mechanical means — including information storage, retrieval systems, artificial intelligence, or large language models (LLMs) — without written permission from the author, except for brief quotations in book reviews. You may share brief quotations with full attribution.

Distribution, reproduction, adaptation, derivative works, integration, upload, or transmission of this content in any form requires the author's prior written permission.

Liability: The author and publisher shall have neither liability nor responsibility to any person or entity regarding loss or damage caused, or alleged to be caused, directly or indirectly, by this content. Trademarks mentioned in this book belong to their respective owners and are used under the doctrine of fair use. This book does not promise or guarantee results.

Printed and produced in the United States of America
Published simultaneously in electronic format

Library of Congress Control Number: 2024927591
ISBN-13: 979-8-9922521-1-8
eBook ISBN: 979-8-9922521-0-1

Visit flourishdirection.com for downloadable resources.

Connect with Flourish Direction and John Arndt:
flourishdirection.com | @thejohnnycakes

Cover and interior design: Nathan McDonald (paxcuriostudio.com)

For Bethany, Mary, Noah and Kelly

Better and deeper question-askers than I've ever been

TABLE OF CONTENTS

Preface	4
1. Who Is The Star Of The Show?	12
2. What Are Open Questions?	30
3. How Do Follow-Up Questions Deepen Connection?	45
4. How Does Body Talk Impact Us?	61
5. What Makes Questions Powerful?	70
6. What To Practice?	78
Prologue	89
Appendix	98
Visually Evocative Questions	99
Kinesthetic-Tangible Questions	101
Deepening Relational Questions	103
Leadership Formational Questions	105

PREFACE

In 2012, the Mayan calendar had us all convinced that the world was going to end. Just in case they got it wrong, I kept myself busy working with a non-profit in South Africa. The focus of the non-profit was church planting. In our context, we helped stir spiritual hunger in people and let them wonder how they might invite their family and friends into a spiritual journey together. Our goal wasn't to tell them what to do, like so many have experienced in Christianity. The approach was discovery-based, supporting them by asking them certain kinds of questions.

This approach had a deep impact on me. It rippled outwards into other areas, causing me to scrutinize and measure the worth of how I was approaching others with advice, suggestions, questions, or data.

I noticed that I offered my opinion quickly and easily as a default setting. Default settings are fine, but aren't tuned for a maximum or specific benefit, just like the default browser on your computer might take you to Google or Yahoo or something you don't use every time you open it. Attuning the default settings to personal preferences, needs, and the specific application is not only helpful but encouraged. I began to realize my default setting needed some help. People sometimes took my opinion seriously, but others discarded it as quickly as I offered it. If someone is in some trouble, offering advice is the logical choice, isn't it? How else could you help them?

In 2012 I began coaching volunteers with our non-profit organization, using Gallup's StrengthsFinder assessment (now called CliftonStrengths), and was thrilled with the experience of bringing some data to a person, a marriage, or a team, and helping them. My knowledge, combined with their test results, meant that I could offer practical insight. I could help them celebrate a unique behavior or perspective, or notice a troubling conflict that stubbornly popped up. Having extensive knowledge of CliftonStrengths meant I brought an expert opinion to so many different situations, and that opinion could help others. I've used CliftonStrengths for growth in self-awareness, personal and leadership development, and to help couples understand each other better. But I began noticing my habit of bringing my expert opinion was leaving the people I was "coaching" out of the conversation quite a bit. Shouldn't they be the authority in their situations?

Why was I doing all the talking?

A few families moved to Africa, Asia, and other regions in this period, and I began calling them regularly to check in with them. After lots of informal talks, my non-profit commissioned me to coach these folks as they settled into really difficult situations. Learning a brand new language, trying to acclimate to a new culture without knowing anyone, dealing with underfunded projects or surviving on scarce financial support, experiencing team conflict, and chronic health challenges — almost everyone was struggling in some way. In those talks, it quickly became evident that my advice for them wasn't the best use of their time. It could help some of them to an extent, but I noticed that if I waded in with my opinion, they might agree with the assessment, but there didn't seem to be a clear sense of progress. If I restrained my opinion and chose to ask more questions, they began giving me feedback about feeling safe to wonder about really hard things, or excited to explore a breakthrough that came up as we spoke (a breakthrough that they stumbled into themselves!).

Why were they getting more out of my questions than my advice?

Lately, the soft skill of communication, and specifically, asking good questions, is getting more and more press by leaders in various industries. Articles, blogs, journals, and social media posts are all honing in on the results that good questions can provide leaders. There are several reasons to get better at listening and asking good questions as a leader:

- Helping employees develop a sense of ownership of company vision and values, for example.
- Decreasing the expectation that the manager, CEO, or department head has to have all the answers, all the time. Inviting others into problem-solving by asking good questions helps share the weight and frees the leader to focus on other issues.
- Building relational trust. When those in authority begin asking open questions, it signals that they care about the opinions and well-being of those they lead. It counters the toxic nature of the domineering leadership trope that so many of us fall into, where the leader's opinion is the only valid one.

> Anna, a pastor, says "I have learned and noticed when I don't ask questions but instead primarily give advice. I do this when I feel afraid. That fear makes me want to control the conversation, control the other person. I feel pressure to be saying the right things.

> When I do ask open questions, I feel free when I leave the conversation. I feel like the other person had thoughtful reflection and self-examination and moments with the Lord directly. I feel blessed and thankful that the people I get to disciple will go for it in answering these questions themselves, and want to know God for themselves. I feel I helped facilitate a more transformative time than had I merely given advice.

Relationships are difficult, especially for leaders who often feel lonely and unable to share their vulnerabilities since they are often expected to embody positivity, non-anxiousness, and steady control all the time. Open, non-threatening questions are an excellent tool to help build trust and manage expectations. If everyone feels heard, it builds connection and gets everything out on the table so everyone can move forward. Ever hear someone say, "That's a good question!" before they pause and explore their answer? That moment of discovery helps them value the relationship, because they know that they'll be prodded to uncover what is in them. They begin to trust their leader as a safe place to wonder about their own opinion or strategy, instead of just using the leader as a faucet for knowledge and advice.

A good question invites discovery. It opens up possibilities. Discovery and open possibilities are gifts to the people around us, and offering them to others yields rewards. I began practicing (and often failing!) in informal ways, like around the dinner table, and in more formal settings, like helping a colleague explore a particularly troubling season in a quiet space for several hours or asking open-ended questions when leading a classroom of adult learners. I noticed a couple of things right away.

First, I'm not particularly good at asking questions. I didn't have an inherent skill that made people remark, "Wow, what an insightful question for a nine-year-old!" I have always been curious, but I'm not particularly adept at turning my wonderings into helpful questions. If you were hoping you were learning this material from the absolute best question-asker you've ever met, you're going to be disappointed. But that's exactly why I started training people on how to ask open and powerful questions in the first place, and why I wrote this book. I knew that if I could learn, so could you!

The second thing I noticed was that if I practiced, I improved. This is good news! Even to this day, if I'm not mindful, I'll slip into my default conversational style, which is heavy on opinion and light on curiosity. I could practice the skill, and I saw improvement. I'm confident you can too. That's what this book is all about. There are several different facets to asking open questions, from mindset to body language, which will make you a better listener. This will have a powerfully positive impact on your relationships, and as those you lead, friends and colleagues trust you more, it will have a deep impact on you. Freeing yourself from needing to have all the right answers is a major step forward in personal and leadership development, as we'll discuss in the first chapter.

After we visit a necessary shift in mindset to make the agendas of others crucial to our conversations in Chapter 1, we'll consider what kinds of questions are helpful to open up conversations. Open questions are the bread and butter for life coaches, therapists, counselors, educators and so many more, particularly for their generous treatment of the person being asked. We'll look together at what open questions are in Chapter 2. Finding a flow in a conversation peppered with open questions can be difficult, so we'll talk about follow-up questions and conversational flow in Chapter 3. But all of our good intentions are for naught if we don't let our body language support our practice of good listening, so prepare to consider how people see you listen. Chapter 4 will be about "body talk," our natural ways of communicating with body language. Questions that make an impact can be elusive, but people practicing this skill manage to find them frequently.

We'll consider what makes questions powerful in Chapter 5 and how to cultivate them in your listening practice. Take heart; you can grow in your skill to be a better listener. Take notes; there will be some discussion about the kind of mindset needed to approach others well in this way. And begin to practice, as it's the only way you'll get better at anything. Chapter 6 will provide some question prompts and exercises you can use to grow in your skill of asking open and powerful questions. The Appendix will offer you actual questions you can use in your day-to-day conversations, organized topically. These questions are based on the list of open and powerful questions I've cultivated over the years but with some help from AI to expand the examples (thanks robots!).

And now, before we dive in, I want you to consider this:

- What would it look like to offer colleagues and friends, spouses and clients, something more than your best advice?
- How might it impact your relationships to grow the skill of deep and empathetic listening?
- What would it look like to be known as a leader that people trust with difficult situations and decisions?
- The skills we discuss in this book will help you get there, help you get to a place where you aren't stressed and anxious, working overtime to solve everyone's problems.
- These skills will help you flourish in every relationship you have.

CHAPTER 1

WHO IS THE STAR OF THE SHOW?

There's no way to get around it. If you're going to get better at listening, you're going to have to pay more attention to the person in front of you than yourself. I wish I could tell you that there's a shortcut to this, but there's not. This is probably the most difficult part of the whole process. The other chapters will be a breeze, once you've started to work on this.

You're probably picking up this book because you want more for your relationships than just your advice. Most likely, you want to be the kind of leader that people trust and find value in your perspective. You want to let your spouse or colleagues know that you are truly listening. You might want to become a better conversationalist and aren't sure how to be more engaging. Maybe you've seen some people ask really good questions that open up conversations into new avenues, and you wonder how you might begin to practice that. You are hoping that the better you get at listening and asking questions, the more positive results you'll see in your life. And it's true. You will see relationships develop more trust and security when people feel heard and understood as you practice the skills on these pages. But a drastic overhaul of your habits isn't going to happen the second you read this book or in the next conversation you have.

My dad loves to remind me of a time when I dove into my lane in a swim competition, made it halfway down, and began to sink. I was seven, and the coach grabbed my shoulders just before I stepped onto the diving block and said, "I meant to go over this with you earlier this week, but your breaststroke is all wrong! You're kicking your legs at the same time as your arm stroke, and they should alternate. Make sure you alternate arms and legs! So pump your arms, then breathe, then legs!" I nodded, but my muscle memory kicked in when I dove in, and I swam like a dysfunctional little froggy, kicking both legs out behind me while pushing my arms in front of me and down to my sides. Halfway across the pool, I remembered what my coach had told me to do, and tried his way. But switching a stroke midstream meant I just came to a stop and started to sink like a stone. I fought my way back to the surface and finished the race dead last.

You too might find yourself drowning at moments when you attempt to retrain muscle memory. But that's why practice is so important. The stakes are much lower in conversation than in swimming, but our sense of shame can sometimes brutally convince us that conversations are just as "sink or swim!" Embarrassment at not having the right thing to say is a communication killer because it can tell the brain that you are in a threatening situation, even if you're just sharing a PowerPoint presentation or chatting with a colleague about a project they're working on. In those moments, it helps to take a deep breath (reminding your body you aren't in a threatening situation) and admit you don't know the information. It also helps to do the patient work of practice in lowkey situations, like conversations with friends, before we attempt to drop our open and powerful questions in a board meeting the first day after you put down this book!

Growth is just trying and failing, learning from observation, and then applying the learning. So, failure is just a step toward progress. Lower your expectations of how good you'll be at this, and try. The final chapter will have some exercises you can try, question prompts you can adopt, and even some troubleshooting advice. The Appendix will have sample questions for you as well. But before all that, we need to talk about how we enter into conversations.

Our first step is to address our ego's attempt to make us the star of every show we're in. This is a difficult step, but necessary. It helps to think of this practice as a service to others, like a good mentor or coach. When you find yourself in a moment where it feels natural to barge into what someone is saying with, "I can relate to that! In fact, this is what I did..." take a breath and think, how would it help them if I turn the conversation back on me right now? It's okay to offer feedback or advice, or even how you can relate, but consider waiting a while before you share it so you aren't jerking the conversation back to yourself.

This is much harder than it appears. Most of us think our advice is helpful, or we wouldn't be sharing it. I've noticed, however, that when we are honest, often lurking behind our sincere desires to help someone with our advice is a plea for some attention. I know I'd love for someone I'm talking with to walk away exclaiming, "Wow! John is amazing. What a clear-headed, observant, and wise guy. I'm going to tell others they should seek his advice! I'll post about how amazing he is on Facebook today!" It's difficult work to expose these types of longings in us and refuse to let them hijack a conversation with their influence.

> Jordan, an employee engagement manager, says, "A lot of times you'll see, especially with mentoring, you're always giving advice, and so it's always directed from the

> person who's doing it. Whereas with questions, it allows the individual to know themselves more. By just asking the right question, it opens up some sort of 'aha' moment that they already know about themselves. All I did was ask a question and let it just land, and so a lot of times that'll just create a self-revelation instead of me saying, 'This is what I think you should do.' A lot of times being a leader can come off as being commanding or directive. Whereas asking good questions and leading people to be internally motivated or inspired has more than impact from my perspective."

Centering the other person in the conversation takes practice but is rewarding for personal growth.

HOW TO CENTER THE OTHER

What do I mean by centering the other person? Setting aside your agenda as the most critical thing in that moment. Not forever — that would rob your friends and colleagues of who you are — but for a few brief moments in conversation, practice making the other person more important to your attention than you.

This is one of the most difficult steps for a leader — you likely have an agenda for your working meetings already, so planning to have some type of personal connection integrated into those can seem impossible, but it's worth it. Once you begin scheduling times of personal connection with those you lead, you'll begin seeing the fruit almost immediately. As people open up to your **nonjudgmental curiosity**, they'll feel bonded to you in deeper ways and will begin thriving in the workplace. Productivity will increase, and relational connection for everyone will deepen as you model a way of prioritizing relationships and emotional health. Those you serve will notice the pleasant and joyful tone. It's worth the effort, worth the tension you'll feel as you work to schedule time to connect with those you lead.

Practically speaking, this comes when you open a conversation with open questions and don't immediately weigh in to share your opinion when they've just shared how they are doing.

Practicing a pause is extremely helpful here. When we feel that impulse to give some feedback, hold it loosely for a few moments in your mind before you blurt it out. A wise friend told me that she always tries to ask **three more questions** when she feels a response bubbling up in her. What a fantastic practice! Imagine you are listening to your coworker complain about their workload, and you think you know what the issue is. You're positive! "Cathy," you want to say, "you just need to take some YouTube tutorials on Excel, you're wasting too much of your time!" But you remember what that guy said in that book about good questions, so you choose to ask a couple more open questions (we'll look at open questions more in the next chapter). You practice a pause, hold onto your sagacious advice, and show your coworker that you have concern for her on your face (we'll get to body language later on as well). "Cathy," you say, "what are you hoping your workload will look like?" Or perhaps you ask, "What would it look like if you've got it under control?" Or, "Cathy, what do you think is blocking you from working well?"

Wow. You let Cathy wonder without barging in with your own experiences or your advice! What would it feel like to release the pressure of "having the right answers" for someone who is struggling?

> Sonja, an accountant, says, "If I'm asked open questions, it helps me get answers for myself. If someone is just giving me advice, it can feel imposing. It can feel like control, like someone is only wanting you to do what they think. Questions help free you."

What would it feel like to hit "pause" on the need to give your opinion and to think about a question that would help that person think their way out of the problem?

Retraining our ego's hunger for affirmation is important, but the other side of this is **reframing others' expectations** of us. When my coworkers know that I'm not going to respond with the "right answer" but that I'm going to help them explore their problem, they're being retrained to expect me to care about their opinions and decisions. It strengthens our relationship because they'll feel that I trust them, and they'll be much more open to bringing problems like that to me because they know, even if only subconsciously, that I'm more invested in them than the problem.

Parker Palmer, author, poet, and educator, helps teachers of adult learners discover that their voice is not the most important one in their classroom. He invites them to consider dialogue as a means of education that depends on trust and relationship instead of knowledge the teacher solely controls. He notes that the typical classroom setting doesn't create room for learning as much as it does for competition between learners.

> Though some classes offered time for discussion, I seldom felt that I was being invited to teach the teacher, or even my fellow students — and seldom did I feel the impulse to try. The classroom was not a place for original inquiry but for imitation of authority,

> not a place of collaboration but of competition between learners. (Palmer, Parker J. *To Know as We Are Known*)

Trusting that everyone in a classroom has experiences, reflections, hopes, and frustrations that could influence everyone else is not easy. It's a revolutionary act that I want to see expanded wildly beyond Palmer's classrooms.

What if you trusted that those you lead had something to teach you?

What if you carried the gift of powerful questions that unlocked treasures in those around you?

It would require a commitment to listening and the courage to not rush to answer every problem. When I led a classroom exploring cross-cultural experiences, theology, and relational dynamics, I began asking open questions that led us to tread deep waters. There was a thrill in asking a question that I knew would provoke the learners and courage to know that none of us knew how we'd answer those questions. It took trust for us to share our thoughts in that space, to wonder together at troubling situations. The best way I knew to create that trust was to continue to walk in my leadership with an open posture that invited discussion, rather than just lecturing. That led to not only fruitful dialogue in the classroom but also students coming to share difficult things with me outside the classroom. They'd offer problems and know that I wouldn't rush to dismiss them because I had already modeled a leadership that trusted their voice.

HOW TO FACILITATE DIALOGUE AS A LEADER?

Imagine you begin to ask open, provocative questions to those you lead. The tension most leaders feel is the concern that conversations will derail, that the answers can't be trusted, and that too many voices will muddy the water with too many opinions. **A team that incorporates dialogue, however, is much stronger than a team that follows the command of a leader.** A dialogue-practiced team shares ownership of their vision and mission and actively problem-solves and plans together, alleviating the often-heavy responsibility that the leader carries. Most leaders know this in theory, but we haven't seen it modeled nearly enough to practice it!

- It starts with the courageous practice of asking open questions and restraining giving your opinion as you hear others respond. Your quiet presence in that moment shows your team that you aren't rushing to tell them the answer as you see it but that their opinion is valuable.
- When others share a point of view that disagrees with what has already been said, take the time to ask

follow-up questions to make sure that everyone fully hears and understands that point of view. This teaches your team that being heard is as important in dialogue as expediency in selecting the right outcome.
- If your team begins to argue about a method, bring them back to consider opportunity before criticism by reminding them you want everyone to have a chance to suggest their perspective. Let them know they'll have their turn to suggest a different perspective.
- Weighing the pros and cons of alternative perspectives helps everyone increase their decision-making skills. Don't be afraid to probe the alternative viewpoint, asking others what they like about it and what potential problems could arise.
- Only when you've felt that you've helped the team fully understand that viewpoint should you ask if anyone else has a suggestion.
- After you've given time for everyone to share, if you need to consider the options, let them know you'll get back to them on how to move forward. If you feel confident about the way forward, thank them for their perspectives and let them know how you will make the decision.

Imagine you hear opinions that won't move your mission forward or that this type of dialogue might waste time — what is the worst that will happen? You will develop the skills to facilitate dialogue without committing to agree with every opinion. You will engender trust in the team as they realize you value their voice. You will be surprised at the solutions that expand your agenda's scope with creativity and fresh ideas, as each person brings with them all their experiences, knowledge, and skillsets. When someone feels you are listening to them, their anxieties are calmed, their sense of belonging is strengthened, and their commitment is deepened.

HOW TO LISTEN WELL

Have you ever had someone listen to your problems, really deeply listen? Not grabbing the reins of the conversation and steering it back to their experiences when you took a pause, but hearing you out completely? Imagine, as you share, the other person is asking more questions, not just for their own curiosity's sake, but to more fully understand you. This experience is not as common as it could be, but it is very fruitful to relationships that experience it. Practicing this skill will not only build your relationships with your team but also prepare you well to facilitate dialogue in a corporate setting by training you to center the other person.

Letting the other person be centered is a gift, and the most simple way to give that gift is to point the agenda back to the other person. Your gift at that moment is to explore what's important to them.

WHAT'S ON THEIR MIND?

Practically speaking, a life coach or therapist can start by giving that gift pretty easily by asking, "What's important to you?" or "What would you like to focus on?" The other person already expects that they'll bring the topic, so they're not surprised that they get the final say on what gets talked about. But in more informal conversations, you can give the gift of the agenda through questions like "What have you been excited about lately?", "How has the last week been for you?" "What was your takeaway from that experience?" and even the innocuous "How was that?"

These questions set the tone for the next few moments, letting the other person know they can make the conversation flow wherever they want to. You'll find out pretty quickly how comfortable they feel going into a topic, depending on all sorts of factors like how urgent their day is, who else is around to eavesdrop, and, significantly, how close they feel to you. Some won't feel as open with you right when you start asking these sorts of questions if they're not sure they can trust you as their leader. It may take time to develop deepening relationships amongst those you serve as a leader, but consistent check-ins with open questions will get you there.

The open-question examples I gave aren't too focused on a right or wrong answer or demand a certain level of intimacy. They give the other person agency to answer however they feel to, and your follow-up questions can give them more space to explore what they're expressing if they'd like. Follow-up questions are really important because they also help clarify for the other person that you aren't just asking a question as a form of greeting, like "What's up?" Helpful follow-up questions let the other person know that you genuinely care about them and their topic, more firmly reminding them that they are centered in these moments.

At this point, you might feel some tension. Consider you are asking Pete about his weekend, and he opens up and shares that it was a bit difficult because he had some unannounced visitors come through and take most of his family's time on Saturday. As you give him some more room to share with a follow-up question like, "What was difficult about that?" and he begins to go into greater detail, a small part of your brain might begin insisting you get to what is important. It starts waving its hands to get your attention and calling out, "We're supposed to go over the IPS reports with Pete, and we have a meeting in just 45 minutes!" That's a tension that's familiar to most of us. We feel the desire to check in relationally with those we lead, but the demands of our work might suffer if we ignore them. The most helpful way I've seen this navigated is by calling attention to the tension and affirming your care for the person. Something like, "Wow, Pete, that sounds tough. I'd be happy to talk about that with you later this afternoon or tomorrow, but at the moment, I know we need to get these annoying reports out of the way. But let's have a coffee if you're up for it so I can hear more about it. Sound good?"

If you created a path for further conversations, congratulations! You've just set up another opportunity to practice open questions! And since you've affirmed to "Pete" that you care enough about him that you'd schedule some time to talk about his troubling weekend, you've already built some trust and expectation.

EMPATHETIC AND COMPASSIONATE LISTENING

Letting someone know that what's important to them is also important to you is one of the best ways to center the other person in the conversation and will let them feel heard. Two other ways of deepening your impact in skillful listening are empathetic listening and compassionate listening. They both allow you to engage with your emotions as you hear the other person's experience.

Imagining what it would feel like for you to be in their shoes is the easiest way into **empathetic listening**. When a coworker begins to describe their horrific vacation experience at a terrible hotel, instead of shifting into problem-solving for them, like pointing out, "Maybe next time...," consider what it feels like to expect a really fun time with family and be disappointed by a corporation. What would it feel like if you were in that experience? Exploring some of the negative emotions that might surface, like frustration, anger, sadness, or disappointment, etc, actually helps you relate to the person who's sharing the story. This can be more difficult than it appears, especially if the feelings are negative or particularly intense.

None of us are comfortable with emotions we regard as negative, so often, when we hear someone sharing their experience with negative emotions, we begin to emotionally disengage and look for ways to dismiss what they were feeling or abruptly change the conversation. As someone is sharing about their terrible hotel experience, this could look like responding, "Well, it doesn't sound like it was that bad," "Well, at least you got to go to the beach," or "That sucks. Huh. Well, I wanted to ask you about where you got your new laptop bag — looks like plenty of room in there for IPS reports." These approaches stem from an increasing discomfort with the other person's negative emotions, and we can try to dismiss our discomfort by dismissing their expressed emotions.

By imagining ourselves in their shoes, we are doing the opposite of these inclinations. We are leaning into the negative response we find in ourselves from what the other person is saying, and we are glancing at the surfacing emotions and recognizing that if we feel like this now, then how much more would they feel like this in that actual situation? It's an exercise to practice empathetic listening. And it's not over when we discover the emotional response to what they are saying. **We have to allow them to see we're being affected by their words.**

This lets them know we are empathizing with them in a meaningful way. It could be as simple as a reflection back, like, "Oh that's terrible! It sounds like you were disappointed/hurt/frustrated. How are you now?" or an empathetic acknowledgment — "I would be so frustrated/mad/sad! How are you handling it?" Notice in both examples, I suggested turning the response back to them. This is critical in centering the other since if we begin to feel a negative emotion as they share, we are at higher risk of yanking the conversation back to us to let them know we feel the same way because last year, when we went on vacation, we... Do you see how easy it is? Of course, you should feel free to share your own experience with them, but just wait a bit so they feel centered in that moment, they feel heard in their telling of it, and they feel your empathy. After you've chatted for a while about them, then feel free to share your own experience.

Compassionate listening carries a different experience for us to practice. We may not have the same type of inner emotional response as in empathetic listening, as we may not be able to relate to some of the experiences or emotions that the other person is sharing. In this case, compassionate listening can help us practice how to hear them and center them well.

Compassionate listening, at its core, is about hearing what someone has been through and showing them compassion or kindness as they share. Instead of relating from a place where you imagine you are feeling what they feel and letting them know you can imagine that, you are intentionally creating a listening space that shows them kindness. This could look like making non-judgmental observations as they share, like, "It sounds like you had expected a lot more of the hotel. Of course, you had such high hopes for a fun time!" Or it can look like treating their story with kindness, like "What a roller coaster you've been on. Fun times at the water park, and then sweltering heat at night in the hotel! That must have been hard to adjust." You can use compassionate questions to help them articulate their story more, like "I wonder how that disappointment affected your whole family?" or "How do you wish your kids or husband would have responded differently?" The goal is for them to know they can share their frustrations, emotions, and needs without feeling judged. This is a wonderful way to center the other.

It's easier for me to practice compassionate listening than empathetic listening. In my work as a coach and spiritual director, I just don't find myself feeling with someone very often. It does happen, and I try to be open to that sort of emotional experience in my deep listening, but it doesn't come very naturally to me. I do find ripe opportunities to treat my clients and friends with compassion, though, letting them know their stories matter, their responses are heard, and they are not judged. I do this most often with open questions, which we'll discuss in the next chapter.

PRACTICE

In a conversation today, practice holding a pause after someone finishes sharing about their day, their work, or their family.

- Take slow breaths and smile or furrow your brow, letting them know you are listening to them. Don't rush to speak, but let them say more if they'd like while you wait.

- Ask two or three questions before you share your perspective. Start with "How did that feel?" or "What was that like?"

- Notice the difference between compassionate and empathetic listening in your conversations. When did you feel moved while someone was sharing? What emotion were you feeling? How were you able to show compassion and kindness when you weren't feeling a particular emotion?

CHAPTER 2

WHAT ARE OPEN QUESTIONS?

When practicing deep listening with friends, colleagues, and family, I use open questions as my default to start conversations — at least to start the conversation. These questions invite the other person to share their thoughts and feelings rather than just giving yes or no answers. For example, instead of asking, "Did you have a good weekend?" I might ask, "What did you get up to this weekend?" Instead of saying, "Do you like Starbuck's new fall flavor drink?" I might ask, "How are you experiencing the change in season?" These questions typically encourage more detailed sharing and lead to richer conversations. Open questions create broader discussions, while closed questions typically bottle answers in a yes or no response.

It's good to avoid yes/no questions whenever possible when you're practicing deep listening. These questions can quickly shut down a conversation and don't give the other person much room to share their perspective. Instead, try to ask questions that encourage them to elaborate and explain their thoughts and feelings. We'll look at follow-up questions in the next chapter, but it's good to know that often, the most fruit in a good conversation happens in the follow-up questions after someone has answered an open question. Don't expect someone to share their deepest pains or brightest hopes when you offer them an open question out of the blue. You're starting to set the tone of the conversation with an open question, not a lawyer trying to pin down the truth or an interviewer grading their response.

There are times when closed questions bring clarity, so we can then move on to exploring deeper issues, as Alfred points out.

> Alfred, a missionary in Asia, says, "I have found that there are useful questions which are not open. For example, I was talking to my friend and he came up with a long diatribe about visas, how it was a problem in his life. And I just sensed that there was some-

thing not right with what he was saying. So I said, 'Is this really your problem?' And he sat there for a moment, and then he said, 'No.' I then asked him, 'How would you feel if you would never have to come back to this country?' And he said, 'Well, mixed feelings.' I was able to pursue the question, and eventually, it came out that he was unhappy with his life at home. He felt that he was not working effectively at home. So we spent a lot of time thinking about how he could increase the power of his work at home. And that came from a question about visas. To help him, I had to make sure that I was chasing the real problem. And so that was a closed question that I asked, but it was a powerful question in the context, and let us use other open questions to explore what he could do about it."

A helpful way to practice changing your questions from closed to open is to ask yourself if they need more than one word to answer. When you sit down next to someone you're leading at the beginning of the week, you might ask them, "Did you like having the extended weekend?" This will lead to a closed answer. They'll answer yes or no. If they're feeling chatty and they're comfortable with you, they may add on why they enjoyed it. But why hope for them to share more? Let them know right away that you are open to hearing about their life. Try changing the question to at least "How was your weekend?" or better, "What kinds of things do you like having extra time for on weekends?" These let your friend know that you care about their thoughts and plans. Practice changing your closed questions to open questions, and you'll open up conversations much more quickly.

LEADING THE WITNESS

Not every question will demonstrate your open-handedness in where the conversation will go. You can ask an open question that can feel closed. I refer to this as "leading the witness." It sounds like you're asking an open question, but really, you are looking for a specific answer. This subtly communicates to the other person that there's a right way to answer and a wrong way. It can increase the pressure on them to answer the right way, and for some of us, it will provoke us to resist answering because it can feel like we're being cornered.

This feeling is amplified by the power dynamic between a leader and someone under her influence. Most of us subtly weigh the opinions of our leaders heavier than friends or coworkers, so we'll automatically try to please our leaders with answers that put us in a good light. If you haven't had time to build the trust that is necessary for honest vulnerability with those you lead, then you'll need to work diligently at keeping your questions from sounding manipulative or assuming too much.

For example, when you chat with someone just before the holidays, you might be tempted to ask, "Isn't it so frustrating to have to fly so far for just a couple of days together?" Imagine if they had spent weeks looking forward to the holiday, and suddenly they feel cornered with a question that assumes they're frustrated. Or worse, they might feel you are inferring that the long travel might affect their work. They won't feel understood, and it may decrease the excitement they had. If they feel like they can challenge the perspective, then they'll automatically be on the defensive, arguing how much they love their family or that they will take care of all their work before they travel. They might assume that you don't care much for family celebrations or think they will not prioritize their work first, which may be false! These assumptions can take place instantaneously, one assumption leading to the other, and are difficult to take back. What's a good open question you could ask them when you chat just before the holidays? What would open the doorways in your conversation, give you a chance to wander around with them and pay attention to the things they might care about? **Take a moment to come up with one.**

What does the question start with? Chances are that it begins with What, Where, Who, Why, When, or How. These often lead to open questions. They're all good, but most people in listening professions tend to avoid Why. Even though it can lead to a great open question, whenever people hear "why," they often assume judgment. If you ask someone you're leading, "Why did it take so long for you to get this done?" it can be perceived as assessing that something is wrong with the amount of time it took. Most people will respond defensively to a "why" question, either blaming someone or something else or defending their actions. This leads to the opposite types of interactions we're hoping for in asking open questions.

So maybe a question like "What were you hoping to see happen when you began the project?" or "What is your ideal way to begin a project like this?" or "How could we get the most out of our time together? What would you like to plan for?" These open up responses, give them a chance to share what they're excited about, hoping for, or what to prioritize.

Take a look at the question you were playing around with. What's its strength? Where is it leading someone? Is it boxing them into a closed response or a defensive response? Is it giving them room to share what they'd like? What could you change in the wording to create more of an open question, if it isn't quite there yet?

What if you're genuinely wanting to know about a subject, but think you might be "leading the witness?" Let's take a complicated subject for most people — religion.

You heard that your colleague had changed religions. There are lots of opportunities for pitfalls when you have a complicated subject that touches on areas you might feel strongly about. So, instead of asking them something like, "Aren't you afraid you'll go to hell?" or "Won't your parents be disappointed?" or "Won't your kids hate missing Temple/Friday prayers/communion (etc., etc.)," try "What led you to such an important decision?" Another great one would be, "What has helped you in this religious transition?" That gives them room to talk about what's been difficult or enjoyable. You don't have to assume that it's been awful or that they've made the wrong decision.

Engaging with coworkers, friends, and family can be tricky when you're talking about beliefs and values. This led to many people demanding that politics and religion stay out of the workplace or dinner table conversation. I believe we can have healthy conversations with people who have a very different set of beliefs as long as we listen compassionately and don't assume. Asking open questions helps us connect and understand each other more deeply, even if we don't agree with a belief or decision someone else has made. Open questions lead to honest dialogue, and that is the bedrock of a healthy civil society, a well-functioning democracy.

GRAB ONE FOR THE ROAD

By now you might be thinking, how on earth am I supposed to come up with a good open question (that doesn't lead to a simple yes/no) that doesn't start with "why," that doesn't "lead the witness" to try and get them to a certain answer I want to hear, all in the moments when I sit down to chat with this colleague?

It can be overwhelming to know where to start. My advice is to grab a good question and stick it in your back pocket (I have some in the Appendix for you!). When I first began this journey of wanting to go deeper into relationships, I wrote down some open questions that I liked, and I would sometimes glance at them before I headed into a coffee shop to sit down with a friend. It's fine to prepare a question to help start the conversation. But according to my trial-and-error, you don't need more than one.

I used to think of three or four good open questions before I met someone for a coffee, and it was too much to try and keep in my head. Sometimes I'd miss what someone was saying because I was thinking about which question to ask next. I found that as I got better at listening, I rarely asked the last several, even if we met for a couple of hours. Once you have someone responding well to a good open question, don't immediately lob another open question that steers the conversation in a different direction! There are different kinds of questions you can ask. The three I'm concerned with for us to understand are introductory questions, follow-up questions, and full-switch questions.

Introductory questions are simple. They get us started. It's as simple as "How are you?" or as complex as "How has your transition from full-time student to stay-at-home dad been?" Introductory questions are great for setting the stage for the conversation, and I would recommend you gather your own list of a couple of questions you find helpful for different situations. You're welcome to borrow some from my list in the Appendix. You don't need more than two when you walk into a conversation, though. The second one will be what we'll call a full-switch question.

Full-switch questions change the course of the conversation. They can sound like, "Yeah, it has been a crazy year for farmers! Hey, I've been meaning to ask you, what was your experience in Europe like this summer?" It could be another question from the list of good open questions you have, or it could be something that surfaces as you're talking, and you realize you want to go another way. Here's my warning: if you throw out full-switch questions too soon, it will look like you didn't care about the first question they were responding to. If you pepper them with too many full-switch questions, it will sound and feel like an interview, or even worse, a cross-examination. I'd suggest no more than three full-switch questions in an hour or so conversation. You will get more natural at asking good questions as you practice, and you'll get a feel for how long it's been talking about one subject and when it's appropriate to naturally turn the conversation with a full switch. Active talkers can use many more full switches when they're talking with each other, but drop an introvert or slow-responder into that conversation, and they can feel overwhelmed and stressed by the pace.

The third category of questions is **follow-up questions**. I've mentioned before that this is where the gold is in the conversation — we'll dig into that treasure in the next chapter. For now, just know it's any question that follows the train of thought based on someone's response to an opening question. For example, "How did that affect you?" is a fantastic follow-up question.

Asking an open question is meant to help you talk more freely and deeply with others, not scare them off. The tone of how we talk is important. You can have Artificial Intelligence ask you a great open question, but it won't make you feel more connected to the chatbot. We'll talk more about body language later on, but the tone of how you ask your open questions is important.

SETTING THE TONE

One of the temptations in looking for an open question is to make it great. To really knock their socks off. It happens to all of us — we want to ask a question that makes them pause and say, "That's a great question." Nothing wrong with that, but our hunt for the right question can take an odious turn if we begin packing the question with qualifications to make it more specific. This still happens to me. Instead of asking, "How did that affect you?" I might make the mistake of asking, "How did you feel that…how did that experience come across, when you think about it now?" They'll be able to answer that, but it's messy. I started to change the question halfway through and qualified it too much at the end with "when you think about it now." A good open question should be **simple** and **succinct**.

I often find myself adding clauses to a question when I realize that my question is not going to get to the heart of what I want to know. I might wonder, "This could be confusing for them, or they're going to take this in a different direction than I want to go." Now I'm learning to pause and let a simple and succinct question sit with them, even if it's not the best question I wanted to ask them. I can always ask them for another one! I am learning to let it go and let them answer, and then if I feel I need to, I can say, "I wonder about this, too — how are you experiencing it now?" Or better yet, get simpler! Don't qualify it, just ask, "How are you experiencing it now?" after they've answered your first question. Let the simple questions stand on their own.

A good open question can be impactful. Sometimes they will be, and sometimes they won't, but it's helpful to realize that you don't need ten impactful questions in an hour-long dialogue with a friend. If you ask one question that might positively impact their thinking at that time, you've given them a gift. If you aim for ten, it will be intense and too overwhelming for them to have a good perspective shift. When I look back at my conversations, **95% of the impactful open questions happened deep in a conversation when I found a follow-up question that related to what they had been sharing**. It's ok to look at the introductory questions as a means of getting into the dialogue rather than being a powerful question that has a positive impact. For example, if I start a conversation with "What would treating your body with love this week look like?" it might be weird, it might come off as "leading the witness" (they might feel I'm assuming they aren't loving their body well), and it most likely will not be grounded in good connection enough for them to answer honestly and thoughtfully. But if a friend has been sharing about how hard her work life has been on her body, and how she's been numbing out to stress by spending hours and hours with Netflix and junk food, then that question suddenly comes alive in the middle of that context. Context is everything for a follow-up question.

Following the flow of these three types of questions is the most helpful way to begin practicing. Choosing a great introductory question, like "How are you?" or even better, "What's your summer been like?" gives them a chance to ease into the conversation. You're letting them open up as much or as little as they'd like. Most people greet each other with a "How are you?" and so most of us answer robotically. Letting them know you aren't just asking because it's polite can be as easy as a gentle follow-up question, like "That sounds stressful. How are you handling it?"

"How are you?" is a fine way to let them test the waters. There are a couple of ways people can respond to that. The brush-off, which is the custom "I'm fine, and you?" and the intense **TMI** (too much information, all too quickly). I pray you experience the wild chaos of that TMI moment and embrace the unsettling inner nervous energy of realizing you have no idea where they are going and what is going to happen next. Let the rest of the world fade as you attend to that moment, that gift. You'll learn about yourself — how you respond, how you make room for them, or how you might retreat at the intensity. But these are rarities. The majority of times you ask gentle introductory questions will elicit a benign response.

Asking these introductory questions not only eases them into the conversation, where you can hopefully connect more authentically, but gives them room to refuse going deeper. This is important — open questions provide deep relational connection and understanding instead of turning you into a cross-examiner. People have the agency to choose how much information they want to divulge to us, and that's wonderful. By respecting their boundaries and comfort level, we create the trust that allows us to be safe enough for someone to share more vulnerably.

After you have led them into a conversation where they realize they can share safely and openly, you could continue with follow-up questions, or pull a full-switch question, one that you sense would lead you both into deeper knowing and sharing. It might arise from the topic that you were talking about, or it might be from a list of good questions you've cultivated. These lead you into open spaces in your dialogue. Remember that your job is not just to ask questions the entire time. Leave that to the professionals, the spiritual directors and coaches, the counselors and cross-examiners.

If you only ask questions, then the tone of the dialogue shifts to become only about them, and you'll miss out on the joy of sharing more deeply and authentically. It can also make your coworkers, or even friends, feel that you are treating them like a project if you only ask questions in every conversation. Give it a good fifteen to twenty minutes before you shift the topic back to you and your understanding, though. You'll get a sense as you practice when it's appropriate to do this, and depending on how long you have to talk with this person, you may give them the attention they need for much longer before you share yourself.

The tone of asking open questions, and the pacing of choosing introductory, follow-up, and full-switch questions are all different for everyone. You'll learn for yourself as you practice with those you lead, or with your partner tonight about when asking about their day. You'll learn for yourself as you meet a friend over a drink and hear about their heartbreak or their new job. Practice makes muscle memory, so you can reach for good questions that begin to surface as you hear someone's vulnerable and honest response. The best preparation for all of this is, as you might guess, follow-up questions.

PRACTICE

Explore open questions in a conversation today.

- Use an open question from the Appendix to help set the tone for a conversation. Try a broad introductory one, like "What's this season been like for you?" or "What are you looking forward to this week/month/year?"

- Start a question with "What" or "How" to keep it nice and open, even if it feels awkward at first.

- Aim to keep them simple and short. If you feel yourself starting to qualify the question (like "...you know, if it's ___ and you are feeling ___"), bite it off if you can! Keep it short and sweet.

CHAPTER 3

HOW DO FOLLOW-UP QUESTIONS DEEPEN CONNECTION?

Being a skillful listener, a good question asker, and an empathetic ear means more than memorizing five great questions to ask a colleague before you come to work in the morning. **There's more to do in skillful, deep listening than just asking a litany of questions.** In the fairy tale about Hansel and Gretel, they leave a trail of breadcrumbs that their father ends up following and saving their lives. Perhaps you may not save a life by asking good questions, but following the breadcrumbs that someone is leaving in a conversation still helps them feel heard and often lets them dive deeper into new learning. Following the breadcrumbs of a conversation will lead to a much more rewarding experience than asking several unrelated open-ended questions, which could make your coworker feel like you are trying to figure out the criteria for how they choose their passwords. Random open questions, one after the other, can be isolating and produce the opposite you are aiming for with your deep listening efforts! This chapter is focused on helping develop your use of follow-up questions and reflective listening for a natural and engaging flow of conversation.

ATTUNED RESPONSE

The best way to start is to pay attention to the initial response. This is where you can discern how ready they are for conversation. As we've seen in the previous chapter, asking a general open question like "How are you finding this summer season?" lets them determine how intimate they want to allow the conversation to go. **The most helpful follow-up question should try to seek clarification of their response or go deeper based on what they've said.** This is where we usually swing the conversation back to ourselves — "Oh, that's just like my family! In fact, when we get together…" Although it is great to share your perspective and let them get to know you more, it will build trust and deepen relationships if you allow them to feel heard a bit longer. Let's say your coworker said, "Summertime is a lovely time for my family! We love traveling to a beach, or we go camping. We look forward to it for months!" To maintain focus on them for a moment, you could ask, "What are some of your favorite summer memories with your family?" or "How is your family time different when you're traveling to a beach or campsite than when you're home?" The first question is broad, so they can choose to answer as intimately or shallowly as they'd like. The second question is a bit deeper into their family culture, so this works best with an already-established relationship where your question wouldn't feel intrusive.

A note on tone — I used "attuned" in the heading for this section to encourage you to keep your questions in line with their tone. It would be awkward to exclaim how much you love summer and then have someone ask you, "What's the worst summer you've ever had?" Our questions should follow the general tone and scope of what someone is offering us, or it will feel like we have an agenda to get something out of their responses, like in my example, proving that summers are not always nice for them.

OPEN-ENDED QUESTIONS

The easiest follow-up questions begin with "how" or "what." If you keep that in mind, you'll begin to discover ways of following up without having to overthink it. "How did you experience that?" is a great one that can be dropped into many different conversations, and "What were you..." or "What did it..." are easy ways to find a question. These simple prompts naturally encourage deeper sharing and reflection. Additionally, they help keep the conversation open and flowing, inviting the other person to elaborate and share more. Unlike closed-ended questions that might lead to simple yes/no answers, "how" and "what" questions create space for the speaker to explore their thoughts and feelings more fully.

EXPLORE EMOTIONS, SELF-REFLECTION, AND MOTIVATIONS

The two most used follow-up questions I use are "How did/does that feel?" and some form of "What do you think about that?" I have facilitated many experiences of deep listening where I am cycling between someone's understanding of their feelings or thoughts. It's an easy step toward their motivations or hopes from there. Unearthing those can be intense at times, but it is almost always worth it. Many of us do not have people in our lives asking us about our feelings, so it is not only surprising to have someone create that space, but it is trust-building.

I have even asked some friends and clients, "How do you feel about that?" right after they have shared about feeling something! Here's an example: "John, I just feel like I'm hurting, like no one is listening when I am trying to point out how terrible that _____ is!" I'll then ask, "How does it feel to be hurting like that?" In that moment, they are being given a chance to consider what it feels like to experience such hurt, and several other feelings and descriptions might come to mind. This can be a very revelatory experience, to discover what they might feel about having such strong feelings.

Hosting that space for them is an honor and privilege, and almost always comes when we are attuned, reflecting, and helping them dive deeper with helpful follow-up questions.

PRACTICING FOLLOW-UPS BEFORE RESPONDING

I mentioned earlier the practice of asking three more follow-up questions before you respond. This is a fantastic way to train yourself to be a better listener — today, tomorrow, as you encounter anyone in your work, choose to practice this. When someone shares what they are doing, how they are feeling, or what they have just finished, force yourself to ask several more follow-up questions. The power of that pause on giving your perspective means that they are centered in the conversation, and often their response negates our opinion. I have found that when I practice this method, the advice I want to give often dissipates as they share. With more information, I realized they had already considered what I was going to suggest, or with the new information, it seemed clear that my advice wouldn't have helped in this situation. This practice is especially meaningful for leaders, as it helps short-circuit unhealthy assumptions we might make.

CONVERSATION FLOW

Keep the conversational flow in mind as you talk. Instead of listing five questions, ask one and explore it together, using a few follow-up questions. In some settings, it might feel natural and appropriate to continue talking about that topic with them for a while, even up to an hour or more! But in other settings, it might feel natural and appropriate to ask just a couple of follow-up questions before you share your perspective and give the other person a chance to change the conversation completely. The flow of the conversation is built around a power dynamic — who is setting the agenda, and how does that power dynamic feel? If someone doesn't feel comfortable sharing intimate details with you, but your follow-up questions seem to insist on vulnerability, then you will fail in your attempt at deep listening. Noting their body language, their decision to stay shallow or broad instead of sharing specific and intimate details, and their suggestion of a new topic will all help you follow the breadcrumbs of the conversation.

You don't want them to feel like you're roughly guiding the conversation, and if you are in any sort of leadership position, they'll naturally be amenable to wanting to go where you go. Paying attention to the natural power dynamic you have will highlight for them the gift of letting them talk about something important to them — it demonstrates you're a leader who cares and who sacrifices your agenda in that moment for their sake.

Learning to handle the natural power dynamic well and paying attention to how someone is responding (both verbally and nonverbally) helps you become a trusted leader and build a healthy relationship.

BE CURIOUS

Many of our good learning moments occur in art, and Apple TV's portrait of the optimistic football coach Ted Lasso can be quite the teacher. His charge to us to "Be Curious, Not Judgmental" will do wonders as we provide deep listening and open questions to others. Showing interest in learning more about others will keep us engaged with what they are sharing and keep us from hijacking the agenda. It protects us from leading them to an outcome we're trying to get them to and gives us a chance to believe the best about someone if we don't know the whole story.

> Jordan, an employee engagement manager, says "Asking open questions also creates clarity. For instance, in a lot of my work has to do with conflict resolution. Just this past week, somebody was telling the other person, well, you're an ego maniac. The person who heard that was like, 'I don't want to be seen as that.' And so, in order

> for me to break that tension, I said, 'What do you mean by ego maniac? Can you describe what that looks like?' Because this individual's interpretation of ego maniac is totally different than this person's interpretation. So it removes some of the opinion and the bias, because then it creates clarity about what the behavior is. The other person can now reason, 'I can control behavior. I can control how I'm potentially moving about and communicating. I can't get over the fact that I've just been labeled an egomaniac, but I can control my behavior.' So to me, that's one example I've seen how asking questions can help create clarity."

USE NONVERBAL CUES

We'll explore this in the next chapter, but what we do with our bodies is important. They will tell the other person if we are interested or if we are asking because we feel we are supposed to. Pay attention to good listeners around you — what are their bodies telling you about their interest in you?

REFLECTIVE LISTENING

One key aspect of deep listening is the ability to reflect what you are hearing. Reflective listening is critical to making sure you understand what they are saying and gives the other a chance to correct you if you misunderstood. It's also a powerful tool to help others deepen their understanding of what they are sharing, as it gives them a chance to hear what they just said out loud. This often looks like repeating back the last several things you heard, as best as you can using their language, so they hear their own words back. I know it sounds like it could be patronizing, but it is a critical skill in letting someone know you are hearing them. For example, Susan ends a brief rant with, "I just wish we didn't have to deal with having a meeting every other day! It bogs down my schedule!" So you lean back a little and repeat, "You just don't want to have to have a meeting every other day because of how it bogs down your schedule." You'll be tempted to add a question there, but practice just letting it sit for a moment sometimes, and Susan might begin to open up more about how office dynamics are affecting her, or how her schedule needs another look to incorporate well with office culture.

Verbal processors, those who don't always know what they think about a topic until they've put language to describe it, appreciate hearing their own words back so they can decide if that's what they "really believe." Verbal processors often test out what they might think by saying it out loud, and so hearing it said back to them can help them affirm or change their opinion on what they've just said.

Internal processors, those who consider topics and land on an opinion before they say anything, appreciate their words being reflected to them as it underscores how they are heard in that moment. When you take the time to reflect back to them what they've shared, they feel cared for and understood because you care about the thoughts they've developed and chosen to share, and so their trust deepens.

How we reflect back to someone what they've said is important. Using a nonjudgmental, open tone and sticking to their own language is really critical to this skill, or it could sound condescending or mocking. Reflective listening is more than just repeating the words you heard. It's a powerful communication technique that helps demonstrate understanding and empathy. Some other aspects of reflective listening are paraphrasing and clarification.

PARAPHRASING

Summarizing what someone has said in our own words can help them know you understand and give them the option of clarifying. Using our language for what they are saying can quickly make someone feel like we've made up our minds about what they are saying, so summarizing is best when it's anchored around words they have chosen. For example, if a coworker has mentioned how nostalgic summer vacations are, but we choose to use the word "fantasy" instead, like "it sounds like summer travel has become a lovely way to escape into the fantasy of the travel you had in your youth," they might feel like we have made a judgment about how they feel about travel. Even summarizing with a word like "routine" for their word "predictable" can have negative connotations for some, so using their language to reflect is wise.

CLARIFICATION

Ask for clarification when you need it. You can use phrases like "Could you tell me more about that?" or "What do you mean by _____ ?" or even, "I want to make sure I understand. Are you saying...?" These help them know that you are trying to understand, and it keeps you from assuming you know the full context or details.

EXPLORING EMOTIONS

This is a powerful technique to highlight what you are hearing. When you point to an emotion you are hearing, it can help them name something they are experiencing.

One tactic that is worth considering is naming the feeling you hear them describing. Chris Voss, author and ex-hostage negotiator, calls this labeling. This tool in conversation gives the other person a chance to agree, disagree, and/or redefine, but it does escalate the chances of misunderstanding. For example, "It sounds like you're frustrated with the situation" can be helpful to name for your coworker, unless they feel that admitting frustration is detrimental or totally incorrect. Guessing at the name of the feeling or thought can easily make someone feel that you are assuming, so only venture to frame a name for what they are experiencing if they are describing it fairly well. Labeling works best when someone is expressing that they are feeling something strongly but are not sure about finding the right word to express it. Then your offer of the label lets them sit with the label and consider their response to it.

The best way of acknowledging emotions without guessing would be to directly ask them, "How are you feeling about that?" and you can also offer, "That would make me feel so frustrated. How are you feeling?"

AVOIDING JUDGMENT

We make snap judgments all the time, and these can be helpful, like when crossing traffic. But in deep listening, judgment kills communication. Think of a time when you sharing about a decision you made with a leader, a trusted friend or a family member who immediately judged you. How did that make you feel? It likely changed what you shared with them and maybe even your relationship.

Shirzad Chamine, author and developer of Positive Intelligence, would call this type of judgmental thinking a "saboteur" and encourage us to practice disrupting that train of thought by a mindful, grounded moment to invite our neural pathways back into a wise and nonjudgmental response. Deep breaths while focusing on a physical sensation for a moment, like rubbing your fingertips together with great attention, can help disrupt the thought pattern of the saboteur and give you a chance to present more calm attention back to the other person.

For example, when a coworker shares they're thinking of leaving their job, our first thoughts might be judgmental: "Are you sure that's wise? What about your income?" or "You're making a huge mistake!" or "You'll regret this — you're being unrealistic about finding better pay/vacation/boss." While these snap judgments might feel accurate to us, imagine receiving such responses when sharing your own decisions. It makes you feel distrusted and invalidated. These judgmental responses create distance between people, even when well-intentioned. Though accuracy might seem important, building trust is essential for healthy relationships — and no one will trust us if we only respond with judgment.

Instead of sharing our opinion on the situation as if we know it is accurate, ask several open, nonjudgmental questions to hear more context. For example, you could ask that coworker, "What is your ideal working environment?" or "What do you need to get the right kind of working situation? How will you get there?" After getting more context, if you feel like their goal isn't grounded enough, you could ask something like, "What do you think is a reasonable step out of this situation?" These types of questions will help you get the context you are missing, and if they haven't thought about the next steps very thoroughly, your questions can help them begin to think through the implications of what they want and what they can achieve. Keeping your tone and questions nonjudgmental will let them know you are a safe person to process these types of scenarios.

Whenever commenting or mirroring back what you are hearing, restraining any sense of judgment is a key part of reflective listening. Stating the words you hear as objectively as possible and asking the other person for more understanding will help keep you from passing judgment on what you are hearing.

POSITIVE REINFORCEMENT

Although not necessary for good reflective listening, it can help deepen relational connection to affirm the other person when they choose to share something with you. For example, "This must be difficult to share. Thanks for your courage." Or "You are being very honest about this situation! Thank you for letting me in." These types of affirmations help them know they are right to trust you and will encourage them to share more in the future.

SILENCE AND PAUSES

Give the other person time to collect their thoughts or sit with a strong statement they just made. Don't rush to fill in the gaps — some of the most revelatory moments happen just after a strong statement is made, and silence follows. In that time, new connections are being made in their head, feelings are being discovered, and possible new pathways open up to move forward. **Don't rush to fill the gaps — embrace them**. This may not always be comfortable, but it is fruitful.

These tips for following the breadcrumbs of what someone is sharing will prepare you to be a better listener and good friend. As you practice paying attention to the power dynamic in a conversation, try your hand at different follow-up questions, and help someone explore their feelings and motivations, you'll notice that you will fail often. That's the pathway of deeper friendship — when friends try to care well for each other, notice when they are failing, and make it right. This is normal and natural, and every "failure" is a learning opportunity for you.

PRACTICE

In a conversation today, stretch your practice with follow-up questions.

- Practice switching around between asking how someone might feel and what they think.

- Aim for at least three follow-up questions after someone has shared something! Notice when you have found the easy conversational flow, even if it's about difficult things — way to go! You're creating a lovely space for a coworker or friend.

- Be curious, not judgmental. Notice when you feel a strong opinion of what they're sharing is right or wrong, and reign in your response using silence or a compassionate answer. You can reflect later on why you had that response, and what the subject means to you, but don't use their act of opening up to you to do that.

CHAPTER 4

HOW CAN WE USE BODY TALK?

The power of presence has been explored in much greater detail than a primer like this, but we must acknowledge its power to heal. It's the difference between having a computer blink the words "How do you feel?" and a friend nod gently, face scrunched in concern, arms held out to hug you as you hear "How do you feel?" The power of presence means we aren't just our thoughts, our open questions, our quizzical nature, but soft bodies and varied facial expressions. Let's explore some helpful tips for being a good listener by using our bodies. Listening to our body talk, and paying attention to others' body talk, is vital for being a deep listener and good communicator.

EYE CONTACT

For the most part, eye contact is a helpful way to indicate that you are interested and engaged. Have you ever begun to explain something that means a great deal to you, only to notice that the person has started to look over your shoulder? Or worse, they picked up their cell phone and started scrolling? It's a disorienting experience, especially if they had asked you something just before they looked away. I find myself trailing off when someone asks me a question and then starts texting on their phone. Disconnected bodies translate that the other person doesn't care about what they're asking, even if that's not true. So we want to use our bodies to listen well, to match our care with our body language. Eye contact is a great start. Staring intensely into their eyes, however, can be off-putting, so I glance away for about 10 seconds now and then, usually when I am talking, so they can have a break in eye contact. If I do this break only when I am talking, it looks like I'm thinking about what I'm saying, and if I stay connected with them while they are talking, it shows them I am interested. I hold a relaxed eye gaze — some have described it as a "soft gaze," where the muscles around my eyes are calm, and my eyelids are in a relaxed (but open!) position.

Practice this "soft gaze" in the mirror — what does it feel like to relax the muscles around your eyes? To try to communicate love with your eyes? Notice how it feels, so you can employ it in conversations.

OPEN POSTURE

When sitting, keep your body relaxed and your shoulders pointed towards the other. This works well when seated across from each other. I've found that some friends don't love feeling "across" from me, so seated near or next to them but turning towards them when they talk can work well too. I try not to cross my arms across my chest, as it can suggest that I am defensive or uncomfortable about something but sometimes clasp my hands across my stomach. I often keep my hands on my knees, with my legs spread and feet on the ground. This posture looks natural and keeps me centered on them. You'll likely find your own relaxed way to be with people, as you practice letting your posture show that your attention is on them.

Look around at good listeners — how do they communicate with their body posture?

LEAN IN

I often lean in when someone shares something more vulnerable or intimate. This lets them know I am tracking not only with what they are saying, but I am emotionally attuned to what they are sharing. I also do this if they have begun to lean forward to let them know I am tracking with them emotionally. Likewise, if they lean back from that position, I might also lean back, signaling that the intensity of that topic is now being alleviated a bit.

NOD AND USE FACIAL EXPRESSIONS

What does your "resting face" convey? When you are not actively pulling at your muscles to smile or frown, what does your face look like? You don't need to be overly concerned with how you look as you talk with others, but if you do know you tend to frown, you can alleviate that at times to produce the proper effect of looking engaged. I often look stoic, withdrawn, and even brooding if I am not paying attention to what my face looks like. So I intentionally smile, lift my eyebrows, and use other facial movements to try and track what I am hearing.

NOTICING THEIR BODY TALK

Noticing when their face lights up or scrunches into a frown is obvious, but what about when they turn their body slightly away from you? Or begin looking away from your eye contact and just look at a wall or the center of the room? I am not an expert in reading body language, but I am getting better at noticing it. If I'm talking with someone I know reasonably well, I'll comment on it and let them have an opportunity to share what they might be feeling. For example, I might say, "I noticed that your face lit up just then. You seemed to be feeling something strongly! What is going on inside of you?" Or "I notice that you seem to be chewing on something, your eyebrows are drawn together like your brain is working overtime. What's going on?" When I notice someone looking away as I'm talking and struggling to make eye contact, I've noticed they might be uncomfortable with what I'm saying, so I usually don't comment. Instead, I redirect where we were going and give them a chance to choose what we talk about next, like "I know I've been going deep into that, and maybe we don't have time for that," or "Maybe there's something else on your mind you'd like to chat about?" Let their body talk be a map for you, to notice and ask about. It'll also keep grounding them in their body, helping them notice that they are feeling something and that it's okay to be feeling those kinds of things around you.

MINIMAL DISTRACTIONS

One of the quickest ways to signal that you are distracted is to glance at your phone. I try to turn my phone on "do not disturb" during important conversations, or at least I'll turn it upside down near me if it's not in my pocket. Continually glancing around might show that I'm losing interest, and fidgeting a lot often indicates boredom. Some of these movements are so natural to us that it might be impossible to stop them completely, so trying to limit them to when you are speaking or asking a question might help a bit.

AVOID INTERRUPTING

How does it feel when someone interrupts you? Even when they want to respond to something you've said, it likely feels dismissing to be interrupted. Allow yourself to be patient. If you notice that you have a response that you don't want to forget, consider quickly jotting down one word that signifies some of the sentiment you were feeling. You might be thinking, "But what if I have more than one thought to what someone is saying?! What if multiple thoughts come?" A patient attitude towards yourself is helpful here. As you let those thoughts come, consider holding one response (writing that word down, if it helps) and letting the rest go. If they are important, you'll likely remember them later.

REGULATE YOUR GESTURES

For those of us who talk with our hands, feel free to be yourself. Use your hand gestures to emphasize your points or to show understanding of what you are hearing, but excessive hand gestures can distract from the conversation.

MANAGE YOUR TONE AND PACE

Loudly exclaiming when you've been quietly speaking can be jarring, and speaking at twice the speed can feel dysregulated. It can be difficult to change your natural speaking pace, but it's good practice to match your pace to theirs. That will deepen the effect of your listening. Feel free to be yourself, but if you keep your tone calm and even as the default, then when you need to exclaim or mumble, the effect will be more powerful.

ON EMPATHY AND DISCERNMENT

Sometimes we will notice a feeling in our body while we are listening to someone. This could be a response of empathetic listening, where we feel in our bodies what we are hearing described. This is a precious gift and might make it difficult for us to hear tough things. To avoid hearing painful things, and then feel those types of things in our bodies, we may try to stay on the surface of our conversations or avoid people we know to be having an especially difficult time. My advice for those of you who are truly deep, empathetic listeners is to follow your instincts. You might not need to be a deep listener to that suffering friend. You might need to spare your body and emotions the trauma they are going through. I trust that your body will let you know that it's okay to engage again with suffering friends. We each have the agency to engage in that kind of deep listening when we need to, and not force ourselves when it doesn't feel right.

Some of us will notice a feeling in our body that may not match what we are hearing — this is a clue that it is not empathetic listening, but some other kind of response is happening. For all kinds of reasons, our bodies will process what we are experiencing in different ways. Someone else's challenge might seem like a crisis to you, or a simple allusion to a story might remind your body of a traumatic experience from childhood. These types of triggers are likely not intended to have such an impact on you by the other, and so your body might begin suffering something while you are hearing someone else share. Again, follow your instincts. You may find that you can hit "snooze" on that feeling to consider after the conversation, and you may find you need to change the subject quickly or remove yourself from the moment, especially if your body is telling you that you are in danger (a physical response that you can't control). Discerning what you need at that moment can be difficult, but the more that we pay attention to our bodies, the easier it becomes to discern our needs.

Giving someone the gift of presence is powerful and healing, and further establishes deep trust. As you become a great listener, you'll become more practiced in using your body language to deepen your impact. You'll also begin to notice how listening is affecting your body and discern how you need to respond to your own needs. The gift of presence is not demanded of you but something you can give just as openly as a question. How might others experience your gift of presence?

PRACTICE

In a conversation today, notice your body talk. After your conversation, how did you:

- Mirror their posture or energy level?

- Use non-verbal cues to let them know you are interested?

- Notice what sorts of feelings you had in your body during the talk? What was your body trying to tell you about your own story?

CHAPTER 5

WHAT MAKES QUESTIONS POWERFUL?

Some experience deep learning when they are being heard. As we share our stories, we discover the thoughts and feelings underneath our experiences, and it can be overwhelming to sort through on our own. That's why the combination of the gift of presence and the gift of open questions is so powerful. And not every question is created equal. Some questions provoke the response, "That's a good question." These types of questions — where we are stopped in our tracks, forced to consider what is beneath the experience or ahead of us — these questions are considered powerful questions.

What makes a question powerful? My definition is that a question is powerful when it evokes clarity, creates greater possibilities, stimulates deep thinking, reveals new learning, and/or generates action. We'll explore some aspects of powerful questions in this chapter.

OPEN-ENDED AND PROVOCATIVE

By now, you know that I would say a powerful question needs to be open-ended. Something powerful to me may not necessarily be powerful to you, so a question that encourages you to elaborate or discover thoughts and feelings will always be more powerful than me telling you about something. It is always much more impactful for the brain to engage with wonder and curiosity than to judge whether someone's opinion is correct or not, so powerful questions initiate the discovery process. The best powerful questions provoke us to consider assumptions and possibilities that we wouldn't have thought about before the question.

RELEVANCE

Those provocative questions almost always come during follow-up, not the first open question you ask. Forget trying to stun someone into new thinking by the first question you ask, and follow the breadcrumbs of their thoughts, feelings, and motivations. It's on the path into their hopes and desires, fears or frustrations that a powerful question will appear to you. These powerful questions speak to specific issues or challenges, making them much more impactful.

It should also be clear at this point that the best open and powerful questions are for their benefit, not yours. Asking a question that affirms your position as wise isn't helpful, but asking a question that provokes new learning or opens up possibilities for them is highly impactful.

CLARITY

A powerful question is clear and easy to understand. Ambiguity or stacked questions can confuse someone, so a powerful question helps them focus on a core issue. This kind of question often brings them clarity, lifting them out of the fog of multiple emotions and thinking. For example, asking your friend who just shared about grieving a major loss, "What are you learning about grief?" is simple, deep, and has profound implications, as opposed to "How are your emotions?" or the stacked "Where has your loss hit you the most? In your work or at home, or is it hard to grieve around your kids? How are they taking it?" Keeping it simple lets them honestly answer as intimately as they'd like, and it often lets them find clarity in their own mind.

REFLECTION IN DEPTH AND COMPLEXITY

Powerful questions help us dive under the surface. They let us hold complicated emotions together, like the exhausted entrepreneur who is asked, "How has stress and rest shaped your work habits?" The power of a question in context is in the discovery of meaning below the surface. In one question like this, the tired creator gets to consider his relationship with stress, his experience of rest, and his habits of labor. Powerful questions help someone self-reflect and gain new learning about their values, beliefs, and behaviors.

FUTURE ORIENTATION

Many powerful questions point to future possibilities and actions. They don't need to be future-oriented, but the nature of powerful questions means that they might have broad implications for future steps and growth. When I was developing a curriculum for a training course, I took my outline to a wise mentor to get his feedback. He asked me, "What would you like the students to walk away having experienced?" It completely reshaped what I was planning. A good powerful question inspires us to imagine what we want, what it could feel like, and the possibilities of what it could become.

CHALLENGE ASSUMPTIONS

It can feel uncomfortable to challenge what someone is saying, but if we can find an open question, our challenge might help them step out of their made-up mind and into possibility. Great powerful questions challenge assumptions because they invite the other to reconsider their perspective. Many of us inherit a way of belief that may be at odds with who we truly are or what we want to build with our lives, and so challenging assumptions help to recalibrate us with curiosity. It can be as simple as asking someone, "How did that season prepare you for this?" as they are complaining about how the last job they had didn't utilize their skillset like their new position. The question challenges the assumption that there was nothing to learn or glean from a negative experience and helps broaden the learning for their new job.

One client came into a coaching conversation stating that she needed help crafting a message she wanted to bring to her boss since she had been very disappointed. As we explored what she wanted, she discovered a challenge to her assumption that the boss needed to meet her needs in a certain way. She discovered something precious through the question, "How do you want to relate to your boss?" She realized that she wanted to bring herself with confidence and honesty to every conflict, not distort her message to meet an unspoken expectation of her boss. Powerful questions reveal our assumptions and challenge us to make our plans without factoring in unhelpful assumptions.

POTENTIAL FOR TRANSFORMATION

One of the most telling signs of a powerful question is the potential for transformative insights. When a question is given in the context of someone's struggle, hopes, or fears, a question can provide a road out of a perceived block toward personal growth. The gift of a way up and out of a struggle is often through personal growth, not just solving a situational problem.

In the earlier example of a client wanting to craft a good message in a potential conflict with her boss, the question "How do you want to relate to your boss?" opened up insight about herself, her motivations, her history, her own understanding of her gifts and merits. Her gaze snapped back to herself, and she saw that she was changing to be someone else for that certain boss. The problem wasn't her boss; it was how she was reacting to the perceived expectations — spoken and lots of unspoken. So she resolved, based on that powerful question, to approach that relationship in a new way and to let herself grow in specific ways.

UNIQUENESS

This example displays another aspect of powerful questions. I could ask, "How do you want to relate to _____?" to a hundred people, and it may impact some, but wash right over others. The uniqueness of a situation, the context of someone's story, and the flow of conversation converge to make a powerful question. If I had started the conversation with that question, it probably wouldn't have had nearly as much impact. Since it was crouched between follow-up questions, and the client had had a chance to explore her reality, the question was pertinent and powerful.

A powerful question is almost always a follow-up to what someone has been sharing — a relevant question that sparks deep contemplation or open possibility. It can bring insights, learning, and helpful change to someone, and shows that you are deeply listening and engaged, not just to them but for them. Listening to what a powerful question might be means you are not just hearing them, but listening in yourself for the question that might unlock some treasure.

PRACTICE

In a conversation today, try using powerful questions. Afterward, reflect on:

- What kinds of questions today generated new possibilities and new action? Were your questions forced to get them to a certain action, or did they wander into the new possibilities based on your open questions?

- How might your questions have been more unique to their situation and still be open? What would you have phrased differently?

- What sorts of follow-up questions helped bring more clarity to your conversation? What was missing to be more relevant or challenge their assumptions?

CHAPTER 6

WHAT TO PRACTICE

I've offered a lot of content so far around the concepts of asking questions that are open and powerful and some listening skills to help you develop to be a better listener. Hopefully, the practice portions at the end of previous chapters helped give you concrete ways to grow. The best way to grow is to practice this approach in your everyday life, so this chapter is about how to help you get better, practically, including looking at a few "roadblocks" you might hit as you start practicing. First, let's look at some exercises you can do today or tomorrow.

PRACTICE WITH A FRIEND

Let your friend know that you are trying to get better at asking questions. Let them know they can share about anything on their mind. Practice asking open and powerful questions to go deeper, and see if you can follow the breadcrumbs with your friend for at least 20 minutes. If they'd like a chance to try, feel free to let them! Afterward, ask your friend about the experience. How did it feel for them? What would have made it smoother or more natural?

USE A QUESTION WHEN FACED WITH A PROBLEM

When someone comes to you with a problem, knowing you'll solve it as a leader, choose to ask an open question instead. This could look like, "What would you do if you could?" or "What are some different ways we could solve this?" You'll be surprised at the gems that will surface if you don't rush to fix it but instead invite them to offer a solution. This also relieves you from the stress of having to have all the right solutions every time.

This is a growth metric for leadership — amplifying the decision-making skills in those you lead and letting yourself shape and guide the responses according to what you know needs to happen. Living in that tension helps you learn patience and stewardship of the power dynamic well and trains others in their leadership development.

QUESTION A FAMILY MEMBER AT DINNER

Over the next week at mealtime, choose a family member to be the one "in the hot seat." Tell them that you are practicing your deep listening skills, so you'd like to just ask them questions about their day, their thoughts, their passions, their emotions, their frustrations... See what you discover by just asking questions!

NOTICE YOUR DEFAULT QUESTIONS

At the end of the conversation with a friend or coworker, write down the types of questions you naturally asked others. Notice what kinds of questions you asked. Note any questions that seemed to have an impact, that opened up the conversation for them to respond and detail what they are thinking or feeling. Note when you asked questions that were mostly closed-ended or you offered advice without getting more context, clarifying, etc. Consider how to improve.

LISTEN TO A STRANGER'S STORY

The next time you're in public — at a grocery store, coffee shop, etc. — strike up a conversation with a stranger. See if you can get them to tell a story just through deep listening and wondering questions. Practice your empathetic listening and active listening skills to make them feel more comfortable.

ASKING QUESTIONS STRATEGICALLY

One key area of growth is finding the question that fits the context that you are in. The following are some ways to help you better appreciate the other person's state and situation so that you aren't misreading any social cues or bulldozing them with a thousand questions that aren't related to what they need.

ASSESS THEIR EMOTIONAL STATE

Before you begin asking questions that might pry into their life, try to gauge the other person's emotional state based on verbal and nonverbal cues. If they seem closed off, upset, irritated, or vulnerable, ask gentle check-in questions first:

- How are you feeling about this?
- Would it help to talk about it right now?
- What do you need right now?

If they appear more neutral or invite you into their situation, you'll feel more free to probe deeper.

CONSIDER THEIR PERSONALITY STYLE

It can help to note how someone typically communicates. This is especially helpful when you start to mirror their language and reflect what you are hearing. For logical or theoretical processors, frame your questions to prompt their analysis and critical thinking:

- What data informs your perspective on this?
- What rationale and evidence can you share regarding your viewpoint?

For interpersonal communicators, help them put into words their feelings, values, and impact on people:

- How do you think each person involved feels about this situation?
- How might this tie to your beliefs or life vision?

These are helpful starting points to communicate more easily with how they process open questions as a default. As you become a better listener and more natural in your conversational flow, consider challenging the assumptions of which type of communicator you are working with. Ask the "logical processor" about how they feel, and ask the "interpersonal communicator" what evidence is around them. It can help to challenge them to access a part of themselves they don't normally describe.

IDENTIFY THEIR LEARNING STYLE

Visual learners appreciate imaginative questions. They respond well to metaphors and visualizing possibilities:

- If this issue manifested itself as a landscape, what would it look like?
- Imagine exploring a vision of the future where this is resolved. What do you see?

Creative questions help spark "out of the box" thinking and can help clarify vision, passion, and other intangibles. More sample questions are in the Appendix under "Visually Evocative Questions." Kinesthetic or experiential learners prefer questions tied to tangible experiences and actions:

- When have you successfully dealt with a situation like this before?
- What small step could you take this week to move forward?

These examples demonstrate ways to strategically personalize and target high-impact questions to individuals' states, traits, and learning preferences. More sample questions are in the Appendix under "Kinesthetic, Tangible Questions."

OPEN QUESTION PROMPTS

Here are some question templates to start plugging into your conversations. Use these prompts to create your questions and immediately put into practice what you've been learning!

GETTING STARTED

- What motivates you to...?
- How do you feel when...?
- What sparks your passion about...?
- What led you to...?

DIVING DEEPER

- What do you make of...?
- What meaning does this have for you?
- What might you gain/lose from...?
- What assumptions frame your thinking about...?

IMAGINING POSSIBILITIES

- Suppose you could...then what might be possible?
- If anything were possible, what would you create?
- How might you envision...?
- What's stirring in you as you consider...?

CHALLENGING PERSPECTIVES

- What might be some other ways to view...?
- How might your assumptions about...be limited?
- What contradictory evidence do you see regarding...?
- What if the opposite were true? Then what?

EXPLORING IMPACTS

- Who does this impact? In what ways?
- How might this change over time if...?
- What ripple effects could occur if...?
- What's the best-case scenario if...? Worst-case?

IDENTIFYING NEXT STEPS

- What first step feels aligned for you?
- What most wants to happen now?
- If anything were possible, what bold step would you take?
- How can you create space for...?

TROUBLESHOOTING

As you practice, you are going to run into obstacles. If only it were just forgetting what question you might ask next! There are several difficulties you might encounter. Let's look at some together.

RESISTANCE TO QUESTIONS

Sometimes, we need to shift the power balance if someone seems reluctant or annoyed. One way to do that is to reframe to a yes/no question to give them more control. For example, "Would you be open to sharing a bit more about your perspective here?" This allows them the agency to not go any further with you. You can also acknowledge their feelings if they seem uncomfortable, like "I don't mean to push too hard, I'm just hoping to better understand." Try to practice empathetic body language and offer to move on. If they decide to open up, they'll let you know.

AWKWARD SILENCES

Most of us don't like silence. As we've seen earlier, it can provoke new learning or let a profound question or answer sink in a bit, so don't avoid them altogether. Try practicing shorter silences, just 8–12 seconds; don't jump in anxiously. Give them space to gather thoughts. When you are sitting in a longer silence, sometimes you might be wondering if they understood the question, or if they are waiting for you to speak. You can clarify so they know you are letting them call the shots on the subject — "I want to make sure I didn't hit a sore spot — does that question feel okay to explore more?" You can also offer to change direction: "We don't need to delve into that right now if you'd rather move on."

GETTING STUCK ON REPEAT

If you ask a question but keep getting the same general answer, reframe it a bit. If that doesn't work, try summarizing their overall feelings and then redirecting to another aspect or topic: "It seems like ultimately you feel very frustrated about the situation... I wonder about..." I often paraphrase or summarize what I'm hearing, then ask them how they feel about it or what they think about it. If it feels like we are hitting a roadblock, I move on. It could be that they don't feel comfortable going there, or it could be that they've already moved on in their head.

MISINTERPRETING THE RESPONSE

Reflecting is helpful to let them know you are listening, and it gives them a chance to clarify if you've heard them wrong. This will happen to you — you might feel a touch of shame at not getting it right. That's ok, that is the reason you were reflecting, so it could be corrected. For example, I might say, "You're feeling some grief at what your holidays now look like..." and they say, "No, it's more like frustration than grief." A quick and short apology might be good, but then let them share more. For example, "Sorry, I may have misread your feelings there. How has the frustration been showing up in your day-to-day?" Ask directly to clarify and slow down your reflections. Don't assume.

LOSING RELEVANCE

Although we like to think of ourselves as amazing at everything we do, chances are you will muddle through a question or three if you are anything like me. If you find yourself rambling or asking something out of context, just acknowledge it. "I got a bit off track with that question, sorry." Then, you can offer another question that seems more relevant. If they seem confused, just back up: "Maybe I should give you more context…/Let me explain a bit more…"

As long as you keep your open posture of wondering rather than assuming, even the roadblocks you hit will only be learning moments for you. Try to remain flexible, responsive, and self-aware. When you admit when a question flops, it shows fallibility and builds connection through vulnerability.

EPILOGUE

ENVISIONING FUTURE POSSIBILITIES

I want you to imagine that you have begun to practice these skills of empathetic and compassionate listening, and those you lead have begun to feel safe enough to talk about their frustrations with their spiritual life or the conflict in their marriage. What would it feel like to rest confidently when someone calls you with an anxious request about a project? You relax and know that you don't have to shoulder everyone else's problem with brainstorming and that you aren't going to co-opt their problems. You ask probing, open questions that lead them back to discover the way forward themselves. They begin to work better, knowing that they have a "thinking partner" who gives "great advice," except you know the advice is just a question that provokes new thinking for them.

Picture a friend asking you out for coffee or beer and letting you know she's going to resign from her job of 30 years to start a new venture, and she isn't looking for advice. She wants help processing the next steps, and she knows that you aren't going to immediately tell her she's making the right or wrong decision. She trusts you. She trusts that you will ask questions that will help her think about what she's not seeing, even consider what she knows so deep in her bones it doesn't come to mind very easily. She knows you'll "kick the tires" of the vehicle she's about to "buy," and she needs that kind of support.

Growing in the skill of asking open, powerful, and empathetic questions is an exercise, and by reading this book, you've begun the process of breaking down the existing patterns that are going to be an obstacle. It's not going to be easy, but your friend with the relational conflict needs you. Your kids need you to help them discern the right steps out of education and into the furious, unrelenting world of vocation. Your work needs you — those you lead know they can count on you to help them break out of rusty routines and into groundbreaking possibilities.

So… what's going to get in your way?

For many of us, it's our ego, as discussed in Chapter 1. Others let stoic listening or judgment block empathy. Some of us just don't like to think quickly enough to try and grab a question out of nowhere and are nervous about trying out new patterns of communication.

The best suggestion I have for you is to not go at this alone. Invite a trusted friend or colleague to check out this material and practice with you. Find a coach or therapist, a spiritual director or mentor who uses open and powerful questions, and ask them for some help. You can thrive in your relationships, and the obstacles aren't insurmountable. It just takes a few good questions to open up the conversation, and then...

You're flourishing.

APPENDIX

VISUALLY EVOCATIVE QUESTIONS

ENVISIONING FUTURE POSSIBILITIES

- If your vision was suddenly unleashed into the world, what could you now see happening?
- Picture yourself five years from now, living fully into your purpose. What does that look like?
- If a miracle occurred overnight, dissolving this issue, how would you first realize it? What would be different that you'd notice?

TAPPING INTO MOTIVATIONS

- If your heart's desire was embodied in a symbol, what would you choose to represent it?
- What might an ice sculpture symbolizing your calling or passion look like if it were next to you now?
- If there were no limits on resources, teams, or skills, what bold dream would you build for the world?

OVERCOMING OBSTACLES

- If the path ahead manifested as a landscape, what topography or challenges can you envision needing to navigate?
- If this problem was a monster, what symbolic actions might you need to defeat it?
- What bridge would you construct to cross this gap or barrier you face? What would it be made of?

REFRAMING ISSUES

- If we saw this issue as a gift instead of a curse, what might it be trying to give or teach you?
- If there was an important lesson embedded at the heart of the situation, what might it be nudging you to grasp?
- What might this conflict or struggle make possible if you leaned into it?

KINESTHETIC, TANGIBLE QUESTIONS

REFERENCING PAST SUCCESS

- Tell me about when you felt you were operating at your best in a similar scenario. What specific actions led to that success?
- When have you navigated a comparable challenge smoothly in the past? What tools or skill sets did you leverage?

ENVISIONING APPLIED SKILLS

- As you think about pursuing this goal, what capabilities that you have would be valuable assets to deploy?
- If you were to break this down into mini-projects, what would be the first hands-on step you'd need to tackle?

IDENTIFYING RESOURCES

- What relationships, connections, or groups could you leverage support and insight from regarding this challenge?
- If you got creative with your existing networks, materials, and environments, what might you be able to prototype or test out?

BRAINSTORMING EXPERIMENTS

- If you had the freedom to try small mini-experiments to chip away at pieces of this issue, what would you test first?
- What might be an incremental, imperfect step you could take this week to move toward your vision?

PROMPT REFLECTION AFTER ACTION

- After each call, meeting, or effort you make towards this goal, take five minutes to log key takeaways. What worked? What didn't?
- On a scale of 1–10, how effective were your tactics? What might have made them a 9 or 10?

DEEPENING RELATIONAL QUESTIONS

PERSONAL LIFE

- What's something you're really passionate about, and how did you discover that passion?
- How do you recharge or unwind after a long day?
- Could you share a significant life lesson or experience that shaped who you are today?

RELATIONSHIP BUILDING

- What do you appreciate most in a friendship/relationship?
- How do you think we could strengthen our connection or communication?
- What's a shared interest or activity you'd like us to explore together?

WORK OR PROFESSIONAL SETTINGS

- What motivated you to pursue your current career path?
- How do you envision your role evolving within the company/team in the future?
- What aspect of your job brings you the most satisfaction or fulfillment?

EMOTIONAL CONNECTION

- When was the last time you felt truly inspired or deeply moved?
- Can you describe a moment that made you feel incredibly proud or accomplished?
- What's something you've learned recently that significantly changed your perspective?

FUTURE ASPIRATIONS

- What's something you've always wanted to try or achieve in the next few years?
- Where do you see yourself in _____, and what steps are you taking to get there?

LEADERSHIP FORMATIONAL QUESTIONS

SELF-REFLECTION ON LEADERSHIP

- What experiences or people have influenced your leadership style the most?
- How do you define effective leadership, and how has your definition evolved?
- What do you consider your greatest strengths as a leader, and how do you leverage them?

LEARNING AND DEVELOPMENT

- Could you share a significant challenge you faced as a leader and how it shaped your approach?
- What books, mentors, or experiences have contributed most to your leadership development?
- In what ways do you actively seek to improve or expand your leadership skills?

VISION AND STRATEGY

- How do you communicate your vision and goals to your team or organization?
- What steps do you take to ensure alignment between your leadership style and the organizational culture?
- How do you balance short-term objectives with long-term vision in your leadership approach?

HANDLING ADVERSITY AND CHANGE

- Can you describe a time when you had to lead through a period of significant change or uncertainty?
- How do you navigate and lead during challenging situations or conflicts within a team?
- What strategies do you employ to foster resilience and adaptability within your team or organization?

EMPOWERING OTHERS

- What methods do you use to empower and motivate your team members or colleagues?
- How do you encourage diversity of thought and inclusivity in your leadership approach?
- Could you share an example of how you've helped someone develop their leadership skills?

PERSONAL GROWTH AND VALUES

- How do your values align with your leadership style and decision-making?
- What role do empathy and emotional intelligence play in your leadership philosophy?
- In what ways do you prioritize continuous growth and learning as a leader?

www.ingramcontent.com/pod-product-compliance
Lightning Source LLC
Chambersburg PA
CBHW062125040426
42337CB00044B/4116